OXFORD UNMASKED;

OR,

AN ATTEMPT TO DESCRIBE SOME OF

THE ABUSES IN THAT UNIVERSITY;

𝔇𝔢𝔡𝔦𝔠𝔞𝔱𝔢𝔡, 𝔴𝔦𝔱𝔥𝔬𝔲𝔱 𝔓𝔢𝔯𝔪𝔦𝔰𝔰𝔦𝔬𝔫,

TO

SIR ROBERT PEEL, BART.

BY

A GRADUATE.

" Hinc tumidi incedunt, hinc publica præmia poscunt."—*Palingen, in Leon,* p. 93.

" —which come to you in sheeps' clothing, but inwardly they are ravening wolves."
St. Matthew, ch. vii.

LONDON:

EFFINGHAM WILSON, 18, BISHOPSGATE-STREET WITHIN.

1842.

TO THE RIGHT HON.

SIR ROBERT PEEL, Bart. M.P.

&c. &c. &c.

Sir,

In your celebrated *Tamworth Mani-festo*, you declared, that you were ready to correct all proved abuses. I am willing to believe, that, in this declaration, you were sincere; and I, therefore, beg leave to dedicate to you this attempt to expose some of the numerous abuses that prevail at Oxford.

I have the honour to be,

Sir,

Your most obedient servant,

THE AUTHOR.

August, 1842.

PREFACE.

THE nature of the following brief Essay is such as will, necessarily, bring down upon its author the animadversions, if not the hatred, of a powerful and, sometimes, not very scrupulous body of men in this great kingdom.

But, praised be Heaven! influential, and, where her apparent interests appear endangered, violent, as the *Church* still is, the days are gone by, when an attack on any of her abuses would prove fatal to the very existence of the man who should attempt it.

The noxious blast of the *Odium Theologicum*, albeit still annoying and dangerous, no longer kills; and thus the fervour of a martyr will be wanting to these pages. Truth, however, and a consciousness of attempting good, will lend their aid; and the result, it is hoped, will be to open the eyes of many, hitherto the blind and deluded admirers of a gorgeous, but injurious, system, and of a false mode of teaching divinity.

Still, in exposing the vices and lashing the abuses of an institution like that of Oxford, in which the Clergy are so deeply interested, and in whose favour the strongest prejudice so widely exists, there must be expected not only the wrath of those whose interests are attacked, but, on the part of many others, much dogged unbelief, or at the least a cold distrust.

But, in an age like this, distinguished for numerous changes and some improvements, millions of our fellow-countrymen read, and think, and judge for themselves; and, what is more, have learnt to express their thoughts and judgment. Besides which, excess of abuse and license has led numberless sufferers to ask themselves why such things should be? And, to such, perhaps,

example and opportunity only are wanted to in-
duce them to expose a system, which has treated
them vilely.

Therefore, it is with sanguine hopes of effecting
some little good, and of commencing an attack to
be followed up, ere long, by far abler hands, that
the Author, from personal experience, now offers
to the public the following remarks.

OXFORD UNMASKED,

ETC. ETC.

" Hinc tumidi incedunt, hinc publica præmia poscunt."

Palingen, in Leon, p. 93.

THE late affair of the Poetry Professorship, or
rather, it should be said, of the trial, whether the
horn of Puseyism was or was not to be exalted,
and the more recent dispute respecting Dr. Hampden, having drawn the attention of the public, in
a more than ordinary degree, to the University of
Oxford, an opportunity is afforded of offering a
few remarks on the system of education, the way
of life, the manners and the men of that vast se-
minary.

The controversies, to which we have alluded,
have, indeed, obtruded themselves amongst the
affairs of the world; occupying the columns of
public journals and forming the subject-matter of
almost every coffee-house discussion; and, it re-

mains to be seen, whether or not, ere long, instead of the success of a mere sect brought to life, cradled and fostered in Oxford, the very existence of that University, at all events in its present shape, shall not be a question.* Such intestine struggles augur no good to a community where abuses abound. Amidst the rancour of party strife the object of blinding the rest of the world is forgotten; the attention of those, who, otherwise, would be thinking of anything else, is drawn and fixed; and changes are preparing, such as, secure as he deems himself in his snuggery, the stall-fed Oxford bigot dreams not of.†

---

* Let it not be supposed for a moment, that we wish the subversion of that time-honoured institution, which has grown with the greatness of this country; but whose prosperity has ripened, to use the language of a Greek tragedian, into a pleurisy. As sacred sounds and sights were wont deeply to impress the mind of the enthusiast Sir Thomas Browne, so the venerable edifice, the solemn bell, the grey tower of *Alma Mater* strike our senses with awe and admiration. And, it is the fear lest abuse and corruption may lead to changes too sudden and too violent, that compels us to speak; for we should mourn the destruction or decay of each antique building and storied pile with almost a keener sense of regret than we now feel anger at their partial desecration.

† And yet we should think that men so well versed in the words of scripture could not fail to remember the saying of Christ himself, " A house divided against itself falleth." But, we fear,

" *Eheu! quantus sudor!*" what toiling, what writing, what preparation, what canvassing have we seen! what hate, what animosity! Their contests, though moral not physical, in violence at any rate come not far short of that of the two rival towns of Egypt.* But where is the meekness, where the humility, where the gentle spirit of Him, whom ye are wont, with clasped hands and upturned eyes, to preach as an example to all men; and whom ye, especially, should imitate in your lives? Alas! I look for them in vain. Amid the tranquil scenes of a village pastor's life, I see a chosen few, who are content to discharge in peace their sacred duties; and, even within the proud

that many of the admonitions and precepts of our Lord fall idly and without impression on the ears of these expounders of Holy Writ and representatives of the Apostles. Did they feel them in their true sense, they would be as *henbane* to them; to use an expression of the witty but licentious Rabelais, similarly applied.

* Inter finitimos vetus, atque antiqua simultas
  Immortale odium et nunquam sanabile vulnus
  Ardet adhuc, Ombos et Tentyra. Summus utrinque
  Inde furor vulgò, quod numina vicinorum
  Odit uterque locus, quum solos credat habendos
  Esse Deos, quos ipse colit.—*Jun. Sat.* xv.

A Williams! a Garbett! is the cry. A Hampden! O churchmen! churchmen! how bitter are your souls! One may, indeed, exclaim, " *Tantæne animis cœlestibus iræ?*"

walls of the University of Oxford, there are some few harmless enthusiasts in piety * or learning. But for the majority ! 'Tis the craft and cunning of the Jesuit, with a pride and intolerance their own. How many has this driven from the pale of our Church to seek refuge in dissent or to abandon themselves to infidelity? What but this has caused so many dissenting chapels to meet the eye? For this, our venerable Church, her touching and beautiful ritual, her simple yet not too bare and harsh forms of worship, the very religion of our fathers is in danger. And this is to be attributed, forsooth! to the evil spirit of the times, to the immorality of the manufacturing districts, to the over-education of the lower classes, the influence of Dissenters, Radicalism, Chartism, Antichrist! aye! to any-

---

* Amongst these are the men, who sometimes proclaim their existence to the world of booksellers or classics, through the medium of a long dissertation on some trifling, neglected point of Greek grammar or prosody ; a treatise on the Apostolical succession, or a small meek volume of mild poetry on religious subjects. Others, of the same class, are still more retiring. These latter may be observed, in vacation time, prowling in academic costume about college-walks, and, ever and anon, stealing an admiring look upwards to some architectural beauty of design or execution amid their beloved college-homes.

They are, for the most part, short-sighted, absent, awkward, rickety, black-gaitered, and harmless, at any rate as individuals ; and are rather of the *Daw* than the *Crow* genus.

thing but the damning truth. But we are led away from the exact point of which we are anxious to treat. We are speaking of Churchmen generally. It is rather to one of their strongholds, their *forcing houses*, if we may use such an expression, that we would direct attention. And here we may remark, that to us it has always been a matter of wonder, why it should, in these days, be considered necessary, that the great founts of national education should be entirely at the distribution and under the control of one class of men: why the waters of learning, rendered turbid and polluted by interest and bigotry, should be thus ladled forth by priestly hands alone.

In the darker ages of England's literature, when learning and science were not deemed essential to the many; when men of letters formed a distinct, and by no means numerous, class, it is easily understood why those, who were mainly instrumental in reviving or preserving science and literature, should alone have superintended the education of others. But now the case is altered; and we cannot see the propriety of indiscriminately submitting the youth of this country to the influence and control of those, who, but too frequently, suffer *religion* to degenerate into *priestcraft*. Far, indeed, be it from us to advocate the absence of due religious exercise and observances from the education of laymen;

such would be an evil far greater than the one we deprecate. But, what we complain of is, that the religious feelings and principles which, previous to their commencement of a college life, most young persons may be supposed and expected to have imbibed from their parents in domestic life or their tutors at school, will, in our great Universities, be, on the one hand, converted into coldness, doubt, contempt, or infidelity; or, on the other, hardened into the pharisaical precision, pride, and vindictive, uncharitable disposition of the formulist and the bigot.

And first, with respect to those at college destined to the Church itself. There is no discipline; the greatest license, in many instances, if not allowed, is winked at and passed over. Until the youthful clergyman has taken his degrees, and is ready for the process of what is there not unfrequently termed "*japanning*," viz. an actual admittance into the clerical profession and the consequent adoption of a sad and sober garb of " staid wis- " dom's hue," he may frequently be seen prominent amid the profligate, the Coryphæus of a Bacchanalian rout, a man of pleasure in every sense of the word. Is this a right preparation for *la vie celibataire,* which a Fellowship requires; or for the exercise of that virtue and self-denial which the life of a Churchman demands? True it is, that a man may, on the occasion of his being ordained, and some, whose irregularities have been caused by example and the violence of their passions, not by actual predisposition to vice, do suddenly pause and effect an alteration in their course of life.* In the phraseology of the world, " they have sown their wild " oats;" their young blood is purged ; and they are prepared, in an incredibly short space of time, to sit in judgment on the indiscretions and vices of which they themselves were just now guilty. Some, from the above causes, others, and there are more of these latter, from prudential motives, alter their conduct. These rapid transitions, or rather metamorphoses, which, from whatever motive, are pretty general, are not, however, likely to be regarded as

---

* We have, indeed, remarked, that it is not unfrequently the custom amongst the young novices of the Church, whose notions of morality are founded somewhat on the principles of the Italian bravo, who slays and pillages in his early days and becomes a devotee in his old age, to make up their minds to exhaust every pleasure during their noviciate and before the fated hour arrives to debar them from at least open profligacy. " Come," they say, " we have but a few years of liberty, let us make the " most of it." Thus it is, that the melancholy worn-out expression, the placid-looking debility, induced by early and constant debauchery and hard living, when all the freshness and vigour of life is departed, so often supplies, in the visage of the Churchman entering on the solemn duties of his profession, the calm, pale, chastened look that may be supposed to refine the countenance of the cloistered ascetic.

sincere; nor are they calculated to inspire in others either respect or confidence.* We ourselves have known the sternest *censor morum* of a college, and for a time, in his official situation, of the whole University, who could excuse nothing, overlook no venial trespass. We think we see him now,—a thin, sneering, sour, Mephistophiles-looking man, whose lean form, resembling Cruikshank's illustration of the man in grey of shadow-selling memory, told not of the good things he loved, listening, with compressed lips and cold, incredulous, air to some, to him insufficient, apology; albeit a *manly*, yet still in his eyes, an *impertinent*, acknowledgment of error. Yet this man was, but a very few years before, a rioter amid the self-same scenes; his name and his offences still extant in a book containing the *boating annals* of his college!†

* For can a man thus suddenly change the sins of his heart for their opposite virtues? Can he thus, as it were by a momentary act of volition, cleanse his soul, after long indulgence, from the foul contaminating spots engendered by unclean living? Can a man say to himself, after being long accustomed to loose the reins of every mad desire, "To-morrow I will cease to be at heart "a sinner"? In the eloquent words of the prophet: " Can the " Ethiopian change his skin, or the leopard his spots?—then may " ye also do good, that are accustomed to do evil."

† For he had been a great "puller" in his day; and the galley-slaves of a racing-boat, during the time of training, are forbidden, under the penalty of fines entered in a book, from indulging in

This, however, is the best side of the picture. 'Tis but a reclaimed thief set to catch his brethren. But there are more abominable instances ; where the very official, chosen to preserve order and decorum and to suppress vice, has been detected by those, whom it was his duty to watch over, in the pursuit of his own guilty pleasures; abusing his office and authority for the vilest purposes. One may indeed exclaim, " *Quis custodes custodiet ?*"

But, supposing this last to be, and we would fain hope that it is, not of frequent occurrence, surely things might be better regulated than to beset with such temptations in their youth those, whose lives should be examples of purity and virtue. Many an embryo priest have we known, whose four or five years as an undergraduate were passed in every excess ;—profanest amid the profane, most dissolute amid the dissolute ; and why should they be allowed a course of life, which their after-destination so strongly condemns ?—But enough of this. Let us now turn to their much vaunted system of education. Doubtless, it may be said, in the vast fund of knowledge, which a man acquires in the University, a compensation is found for every abuse. But

any intemperance or debauchery which might tend to impair their vigour ; a circumstance decidedly in favour of " the oar" were it of any avail, which it was not in this case, nor is generally, amongst these young *Corinthians* of the Church.

what do they teach? Why, literally, nothing, beyond something of what they miscal " *divinity*," of which more anon; and at best a little of Aristotle's and Plato's philosophy, wretchedly garbled; logic by rote; and the INFALLIBILITY OF THE CHURCH!* Such, truly, is the course of study at Oxford, prescribed by college tutors. Alas! and such is what is styled " a liberal education"!

It is true, there are chapels to attend, more or less, according as a man is obnoxious or not to the powers that be, or a fit subject for persecution. But as to attending daily chapel in itself, it is little better than a remnant of monkish custom. What is the effect of these *vain repetitions*, this " *adulteration* of divine worship," let us ask? We hesitate not to say that they affect, with disgust for sacred duties, the most well-meaning mind. Observe the sleepy frown, listen to the muttered curse, the impatient whisper of the morning, whilst the dull-eyed tutor mumbles, heavily, through the service; or the eager sportsman, among the juniors, as rapidly gallops through the lesson

---

* I might add, that some lessons in the great world are taught;—no where better. For instance, that wealth and rank are idols before which all must bow down; that interest is superior to merit; and that the memorable line of Juvenal should be well impressed on the minds of needy sinners,

" *Dat veniam corvis, vexat censura columbas.*"

for the day. And see the flushed and excited mob
of undergraduates reeling in from the wine party to
evening service,—the obscene jest still on the lip
and the scarcely suppressed laughter continually.
bursting forth. And, perhaps, now, the service is
performed by one fresh from the heated atmosphere
of the *common-room*, his brain stupified with rough
port wine; he reads as much from memory as by
use of his visual organs, and stutters forth apace
the earnest prayer of faith, hope, and penitence,
anxious to rejoin the grave and steady debauch of
the seniors. "*Ingrediuntur cum hâc maculâ tem-*
"*plum Dei viventis; templum sanctum Dei pol-*
"*luentes, judicium multiplex accepturi; quod et*
"*tam gravissimas conscientias gerunt et nihilominùs*
"*se ingerunt in sanctuarium Dei*," saith the Abbé
St. Bernard in one of his sermons, speaking of the
abuses of the clergy of his time; and it must be
confessed that these words oft find their application to the letter in the English Universities. Not
that, were the customs of college life, the *genius loci*,
different, such daily offices of religion would not
be fitting, in a somewhat modified form as to dura-
tion; but, in a place of such licence, the morning
and evening orisons of chapel were "better honoured
in the breach than the observance." Then for the
Divinity lectures, which, besides being delivered in
the most careless and lax manner imaginable, are

generally but the *extempore* prosings, nay *drivellings,* of men, who have no incitement to excel or take pains, beyond the honourable one of doing their duty ; seldom found very strong and urgent in the breast of an Oxford *Don.*

Imagine men, many of them capable of deep reflection and at an age of ardent inquiry, hearing and receiving, instead of lofty tenets of theology and

" Divine philosophy,
" Not harsh and crabbed, as dull fools suppose,
" But musical as is Apollo's lyre,"

the " most lame and impotent conclusions " of a " first class man of his day," touching and concerning the important fact, whether there were *two* or *three* women who beheld our Lord on the day of his resurrection ; whether they were all *Marys,* and what relation to each other ! and this to form the burden of three or four consecutive lectures ; where not only daily attendance was insisted upon, but the most unslumbering attention. Oh, that lecture ! it was enough to benumb all the faculties of the mind. Or, fancy being obliged to listen, for a mortal hour, to a multiplicity of types of our Saviour and the Gospel dispensation, extracted by the muddy yet fertile brain of another *inspired teacher** of youth; the correctness and aptitude of

---

* Gifted Mr. ———! Thy faculty, for seeing meanings of this kind where none exist, is not surpassed by the well-known

which no one but himself could see.* Think how
important a point and delicate withal, to know the
exact number of days of the purification of women,
under different circumstances, according to the
Levitical law ;† and consider the *Trenck-like* exercise
of memory in repeating all the names of all the
kings of Judah and Israel, in chronological order,
or recounting how many sons or nephews of *Jair*,
Ibzan, and *Abdon* there were who rode upon ass-
colts; not to speak of the necessity of being

story of the single non-existent hair of the Virgin Mary, which
all who pretended to faith had power to see,—each accession of
belief adding a microscopic lens to magnify the air-drawn vision.
O, most philosophical absurdity-monger! what bounds shall we
assign to thy quaint, Quixotical curvettings, prancings, and
caperings in the regions of fancy, to thy deep cogitations and
reflections, υπερ ονου σκιας ?

* According to this man, every mention made of water in the
Old Testament, from all the seas and rivers spoken of, and the
mist that went up from the earth, in the second chapter of Genesis,
to the minutest drop squeezed from Gideon's fleece and the
miraculous stream from Sampson's jaw-bone of an ass, plainly
heralded the baptism of regeneration ! Every kettle, pot, or pan,
too, in the Israelitish camp, or framed by King Solomon's cunning
artificers, had a peculiar and important signification in connexion
with the Gospel dispensation. How this gentleman revelled in
Revelations, we forbear to tell.

† Why, this almost challenges comparison with the *theological
and moral* (?) works of Bailey, De la Hogue, Cambassutius,
&c. &c. which form part of the delectable studies of Maynooth
College. *Proh Pudor !*—Oxford !

thoroughly master of the histories of *Maher-shahal-hash-baz;* or the valiant giant-killing men mentioned in the books of Kings, and of such things as the country, lineage, and times of *Uz and Buz* his brother !!! *

We remember the father of a young man at —— College, Oxford, entering his son's rooms and taking up an *Analysis Book*, as it is called, containing notes of a lecture on *divinity* given by an *eminent* (?) professor of that University. Mercy on us! how the worthy gentleman stared, as he contemplated the nature of his son's studies. For dissipation he had been prepared,—he had heard of it. For expense, he had already suffered. For the absence of all study, he had had some reason to suspect it. But for THIS! to find a young man,

---

* There was a strange point, too, which we must commemorate; for on it great stress was laid, viz. " that in tracing the genealogy " of our Saviour, it may be observed, that on the female side, the " women particularly mentioned were not of the most spotless " reputation; as, for instance, Bath-sheba, Rahab the harlot, " and the unfortunate daughter-in-law of Judah." For what good purpose such facts as these should be especially impressed upon the youthful mind, let the Oxonian doctor answer. Should this fact be doubted by any one not conversant in University lore, we can only say, *Crede experto.* It corresponds, however, with a certain prurient hankering after questions more than bordering on the indelicate, before alluded to, and conspicuous amidst these Reverend cultivators of the young idea.

who had distinguished himself in some degree by
his literary efforts, previous to his entering into
college life, employed in carefully penning down,
without any exercise of intellect, imagination, or
even of memory, a series of trivial facts, the least
absurd of which would be unworthy of the mistress
or pupil of a Sunday school! Poor man! he almost
raved! We will not take upon ourselves to say
that he did not swear a round oath. If he did, we
doubt not but that, like that of Sterne's hero, it
will be excused and blotted out by the recording
angel.

O Religion! whose proudest temple is in the
hearts of those of an humble and contrite spirit,—
who inhabitest Heaven, but despisest not the
meanest cottage,—thou, who leadest us from nature up to nature's God, and, who, in the sacred
pages of Revelation, hast taught us " to visit the
" fatherless and widow in their affliction and to
" keep ourselves unspotted from the world," how
is thy sacred name perverted and abused at Oxford!

What shall we say of the Classical Lectures, but
that they are the most desultory, imperfect, and
useless conceivable? We never, during our whole
experience as an Undergraduate, met with more
than one instance to the contrary. Shall we tell
of one man, who got through ten lines of Cicero's
letters to Atticus in about as many weeks? How,
then, was the thing kept up? Why, by a dropping

fire, with now and then a dead silence, of small conceptions and questions of the worthy lecturer, as to the force of small prepositions and adverbs, and a kind of mixed babble or *small talk*, about the arrangement of Cicero's sentences and his country villa. Another Lecturer, a kind of enthusiast in his way, used to require his class, on pain of his sovereign displeasure, to translate Greek plays into *blank verse*, on the spur of the moment. No one, not present, can conceive how ridiculous the affair used to be ; and yet he never relaxed in his efforts to make twenty-four very unpoetical and rebellious young gentlemen not only poets, but *improvisatori!* Shall we tell how the same man was eloquent, at another time, on Greek prepositions and particles? How he spoke long of περί, ἐπί, ὑπό, and πρός, and was graciously pleased with a pupil who cunningly entered into the *spirit* of the thing, and illustrated ἐπί by a drawing of a tea-kettle *on* the fire, and παρά by a representation of one hissing *by its side ;* such as the chambers of every Oxonian display. We distinctly remember him, too, in commencing a discourse on verbal terminations, in explanation of some incomprehensible and, apparently, very silly theory of his own, saying very gravely, " as, for instance, λαμβ- ανω, I am a lamb!!"—a wolf rather, we thought, in sheep's clothing. Would such gross absurdities be tolerated elsewhere? And then the mockery of the weekly essay, or piece of Latin composition. Why that which would disgrace a school-boy in his first year is not objected to.

We know one man, who constantly sent in a blank book: he was never detected, or at least reprimanded. Another had a sort of theme of all work: for, let the subject be what it might, it always passed current. And now we have a pretty correct idea of Oxford studies, at least of those prescribed.

To be sure, as far as he is not interrupted by these and other things, a man *may* read as much as he pleases; but then he has every temptation not to do so, as we shall shortly demonstrate.

It is not only the fox-hunting *fast-man*, who happens to be kept from the pleasures of the chace by a little appointment with a tutor, who, to show his authority merely, will not be denied, who complains; but *reading-men*, by which is meant that unfortunate class so often wasting health and energy for the uncertain and ill-adjudged rewards of the schools, where, even in success, the end seldom justifies the means, have as frequently lamented, in our hearing, the unprofitable and troublesome nature of college lectures, which break in on their real studies.

Here let us observe, that it is neither a classical nor a religious education we object to; but the mistaken, expensive, imperfect, useless, nay, childish and mischievous, mode in use at Oxford, under the pretence of imparting them. Besides, there are many things of the highest importance, which are entirely neglected and almost suppressed at Oxford: we need hardly say all science, the modern languages, the belles lettres, and, above all, morality and the sublime nature and attributes of the Supreme Being, as contra-distinguished from *dogmatical assumption* and *verbal mysticism.*

We consider the classics, as but a foundation for the superstructure of knowledge. They are a ground-work for other languages; they contain great and surpassing beauties, and fine, though exploded, systems of philosophy; but, after all, they bestow little more than a mere knowledge of words. Now the Ecclesiastics, who teach at Oxford, look with jealousy on all other acquirements, but those, which are merely classical and verbal. And why? Must we suppose that the churchman has a finer perception of the beauties of the Latin and Greek tongues, than all other men? that he has juster notions of their utility, than all the world besides? No! but his fear is, that his vocation may be called in question; that his " occupation would be gone;" that the hold he has on the rising generation would be loosened, were he not to teach that divinity, as *he* explains it, and the classics are all in all. The Classic Divinity, therefore, is the idol before which he would have all men bow down. It is his *Ephesian Diana*. He both furnishes the *silver shrines*, and, as the minister of the Temple, has power to enthral the minds of men destined not only to the Church but to every other profession. For this reason, he decries and discourages application to all other literature, to practical science, to the modern languages, nay even to what is, in his opinion, too diffuse a knowledge of our own authors. For this end, a man is sent into the great world, ignorant how to live in it. Why, in practical knowledge, in the management of property of every description, in the *savoir faire* of a man who is to make his way, out of leading-strings, a lawyer's clerk, a counting-house *elegant*, a very shop-boy, who borrows a little of his master's time, or who employs his own, like Franklin, to read popular writings and the literature of the day, would leave the Oxonian far behind.*

When, some time ago, we heard that it was pro-

---

* This is one of the reasons that so many men, who have received an University education, and whose prospects were, on their leaving college, good, sink so very low in the world, prostitute whatever talents they possess in every possible way, and commit themselves so frequently by various indiscretions. They enter upon the vast stage of life with false impressions and erroneous views, without prudence or available knowledge.

posed to apply part of the funds, collected for and subscribed to the *Times Testimonial*, to the purposes of college endowments at Oxford, we thought that, as it is a notorious fact, that nine-tenths or more of the men, who leave Oxford with a degree, are in blissful ignorance of all things connected with and relating to money affairs, (" save *spending it*, quoth our uncle Toby,") we would humbly suggest, that the money presented to the *Times* for the laudable exertions of that journal, in defence of her Majesty's lieges from fraud and ruin, should not be applied to the benefit of men, whose sphere of acting and thinking is so very far removed from things of this nature. At any rate, that it would be prudent, considering the alarming schisms and struggles, rife in Oxford, to invest the money safely, till it be seen how matters are determined there. It would be well to know, whether a colony of young *Puseyites* is to be planted thereby; or whether the stronghold of their evangelical and *tolerant* opponents is to be fortified. Whether the money is to be laid out for the education of pupils versed in Den's Theology, or whether the old leaven of their Pharisaical antagonists is to be increased. We, however, would have proposed a more decisive plan for escaping the dilemma. We would have given it to the London University. They are in want of funds to strengthen and complete that unpampered, healthy, and excellent institution. Such a donation might be of some service beyond the mere enriching of a place, whose chief remaining pride is to send forth to the world the names of *Newman* and *Pusey;* or of those " *mighty masters*" of the sacred lyre, whose rival pretensions, as versifiers of Church doctrines, have lately caused so much discord,—*a Williams* and *a Garbett!*

But, there is another charge besides that of this educational farce. We allude to the gross, unparalleled favouritism, which prevails throughout, in the personal conduct of college authorities towards different individuals, in the adjudication of the University prizes, in the contests for scholarships and fellowships, and even in the schools.

And, first, as to the bearing of these people towards different classes and individuals ; and the various degrees of liberty and license enjoyed by *this* man and *that*. And here we may observe, that undergraduates at Oxford may be divided, with reference to the system of the University, into several classes ; who are subjected to different treatment accordingly.

The great secret of all the abuses at Oxford is this, that nothing is done there without a reference to *the upholding of the system*. Why do they not, why have they not, long since, put an end to the monstrous but universal custom of running into

debt,* which ruins for life, at life's very threshold,
so many unfortunate collegians, and is so detri-
mental in various degrees to all? Because they
think it advantageous to the city and *themselves;*—
a point which we may probably recur to hereafter.
Why do they suffer the University to be the vortex

---

* We had intended to say a great deal here about this frightful
and calamitous system. But we see, with pleasure, that complaints against it are finding their way into the columns of one of
our most influential journals. The writer of an indignant letter
in the *Times* expresses his wonder, that the University authorities
have it not in their *power* to check this evil. " Is the University so fallen, so abject?" he says. Let him read the explanation
we give, and cease to hope, that authorities so corrupt will wil-
lingly adopt measures, which a justly incensed public will ere
long insist upon. We understand, that it is not the wish of the
majority of the tradesmen of the town to keep up the credit
system. They are forced into it, and it often proves ruinous to
them. As to the trash talked about young men withstanding
such temptations, and deserving to pay the penalty of their in-
discretion; we all know how prone youthful natures are to im-
prudence in money matters; and why, let us ask, is such an
experimentum crucis necessary in a place of education, where
the youthful mind ought to be fenced round and guarded from
evil and trained to good, not exposed to trials and danger? Besides, it is not these unhappy boys who suffer alone; but their
parents, their families. Let us recommend to the inquiring, on
this point, the perusal of a highly interesting book, in the seduc-
tive shape of a novel,—we mean Lockhart's *Reginald Dalton.*
There, the misery arising from this temptation is powerfully and
truly exhibited.

of so much dissipation, prodigality, and excess?
Why the scene of such a variety of amusement and
pleasures? Because thereby the young nobleman
and wealthy gentleman-commoner are ingratiated.
THEY have their fling; and, finding it a very plea-
sant sort of place for two or three years, where
there is little or nothing to tax their scanty brains,
and where, to use their own slang phraseology,
there is " *lots of life*,"* they not only speak well
of it, but lend it their after-support and influence;
and, when time has mellowed down their remem-
brance of its vices into a sort of vague recol-
lection of something full of pleasure and excite-
ment, they sigh as they think of some bygone
frolic and their own long past capacity of enjoy-
ment; and, complacently, send their sons to figure
in scenes of like dissipation;—to run the same
gauntlet of dangerous follies and excesses; and to
fill anew the halls, chapels, and long purses of the,
to *them*, smiling and benignant college despots.
Under such circumstances, we cannot wonder, instead of that delightful impartiality with which, in
many foreign universities, both prince, peer, and
peasant are treated by the authorities, men at Oxford are caressed and looked upon as chartered

---

* Singular how language is perverted by these *insects*, these
Lilliputian minds. They call their round of empty pursuits LIFE,
par excellence LIFE! Truly, as Ariphron, the Sicyonian, saith,
ʹΑΒΙʹΟΣ ΒΙʹΟΣ, ΒΙʹΟΣ ΑΒΙʹΩΤΟΣ.

libertines by the tuft-hunting tutor or time-serving
Head of a college, or roughly handled and re-
stricted from all liberty by the stern *Proctor* or
malignant *Don*, according to their rank, wealth,
and family influence on the one hand, or corres-
ponding want of fortune or friends on the other.
Nothing else but the most extraordinary talent, or
rather scholarship, directed precisely in the course
pointed out by his college, so that he be expected
to gain it credit by cutting a figure in the schools ;*
or the fact that he is intended for the Church, for
one of themselves, combined with the most abject
servility and the most persevering toadyism, will
save a man from persecution. Let a youth have
gained his previous education elsewhere, than in
one of the University nurseries ; let him select a
tutor for himself, or prosecute his studies unaided
and unnoticed, and if he display in the schools the

---

* Let us tell the story of a man of rare talent and learning
combined, whom we knew ourselves. His family expectations
were good ; and, being looked upon as a certain *first class*, he
was allowed every license:—*to cut chapels* without end, to absent
himself from college all night and from lectures all day ; and was
encouraged in impertinence and familiarity by his superiors. See
the end. His health gave way. He took merely a *second class*.
His father shortly after was ruined ; and he himself went down
to the University to gain his living as a tutor ; but, in three days,
was ignominiously expelled for a simple frolic, which, before, would
have passed without notice. To whom may his ruin be attributed ?
Has he not cause to curse Oxford and her system in his heart ?

elegant scholarship of Milton, combined with the
critical learning of Scaliger and the mathematical
acumen of a Newton, it shall avail him nothing.
So little do they like a man who dares to think or
act for himself. " *Il suffit que ma méthode ne soit*
" *point la méthode reçue, pour que je sois contredit,*
" *démenti, hué, berné, sifflé, persécuté, et peut-être*
" *lapidé,*" says some French writer. Such is the
feeling and conduct exhibited by these UPHOLDERS
OF A SYSTEM.

Again, it was said, some time ago, in the Clubs
of London, where such things are discussed and
canvassed, that in future, after the decision of the
case of Mr. Elton, young " aspirants" of the navy
must no longer consider themselves as gentlemen;
for it was evident that they were no longer to be
treated as such. But what would be said, if the
overbearing insolence of some of these Oxford ba-
shaws were generally known; why they hesitate
not, without the trouble of any inquiry, to give the
lie direct, in the most offensive manner, to a young
man. And woe be to his prospects, as far as they
can influence them, if he should rebel or treat such
conduct with the indignation it deserves.

One instance of this intolerable and vindictive spirit
will scarcely be amiss; before we draw our observa-
tions to a close. There is so much to find fault with,
and facts crowd into our memory so rapidly, that

we scarcely know of which to avail ourselves first. But we hope to renew the charge, ere long, with re-doubled vigour, and to touch upon a variety of points, that we have of necessity left unmentioned. Now to our story:—A young Oxonian, an intimate friend of ours, who had served a considerable portion of his time at **** College, without drawing upon himself either odium or even remark, chanced, in riding out one day, to pass, in a by-lane, the superior of his college; who had been lately elected to that dignity, and whose person, in consequence, was not known to the luckless wight, as he cantered merrily by. A day or two after, he was summoned into the awful presence of this truly *little great* man; and, after having been kept waiting, in the depth of winter, for three-quarters of an hour, without a fire, (it was late in the evening by the bye,) behold! he is sternly reproved for his " *indecent*," " *unaca-* " *demical*," and " *ungentlemanly*" conduct. Our hero having apologized in vain, alleging, what was truly the case, that he was short-sighted, and that he was also ignorant of the person of his accuser; and having said that he had always studied to pay due attention and respect to his college superiors, he was still yet treated with the greatest contumely, until in turn he felt excited, and remonstrated warmly. " Ha! are you going into the Church, " sir," quoth the *don*, savagely malicious, " be-

" cause if you are, we shall refuse you any testi-
" monials." " No, sir, I am not," responded the
culprit. " I don't believe you, sir," said the other.
" Indeed it is the case, sir," replied the *lamb*,
rising, " and you have neither reason nor right
" thus to doubt my word." " Sir," rejoined the
WOLF, " that *may* or may *not* be the case, but at
" any rate we'll have an eye on you, and if you
" *should* alter your intentions, we shall refuse you
" any testimonials ; you had better not want them.
" We'll stop you, sir. Take care, sir, take care,
" that I don't catch you tripping." He then com-
menced a quarter of an hour's coarse *tirade* against
the astonished youth ; accusing him of every thing
rebellious and improper ; although, from the superior's recent arrival, he could pretend to no knowledge of the young man's character ; who was, as
it happened, previously in good repute with all the
tutors, and especially with the immediate prede-
cessor of this very man. Would it be believed
that, after this, the unoffending undergraduate had
not a moment's peace ; that every thing was turned
against him ; that all the tutors joined in the cry to
hunt him down ; that the college was made almost
too hot to hold him ; and that, finally, they had
the hardihood to threaten to use their influence to
get him *plucked;* a circumstance which he learnt,

much to his encouragement, a day only previous to
his going into the schools for his degree.

Now, is not a change wanted in a place, where a
young man thus runs the chance of having every
prospect in life blasted by the wanton and virulent
barbarity of such a stilted blockhead, as the man of
whom we have just spoken? In the above case, all
the venom, all the malice was happily innocuous.
Our friend, fortunately, was not destined to the
Church: he was independent of the University.
But we have known, nay, we even now know, melancholy cases; where men of talent and engaging
manners, the courted of society and the beloved of
their companions, have been thrown upon the world;
without a resource, unfit to struggle in it, by ca-
price and tyranny, such as we have mentioned.
Think you, that the conceited lordling and the self-
sufficient heir to hundreds of thousands are treated
thus? No; perhaps, when the playful aristocrat
has proceeded too far in his pranks, and has indulged
in such an intellectual amusement as pulling an
aged and corpulent master of arts out of his downy
couch, in the middle of the night, and dragged his
rheumatic or gouty limbs across the snow-covered
quadrangle, fracturing a *scout's* skull, or serenading
the Head of the college with a mixed concert of
bugles, cornopeans, hunting and tandem horns, on

such an occasion as the *accouchement* of his wife, then the thunders of the *common-room council* may fulminate; in the shape of an imposition, written by the accommodating and lettered *barber's* boy or bookseller's apprentice for a few shillings; or the dread sentence of rustication to the paternal hall or castle till the end of term, not altogether unapproved of by this glorious martyr to discipline, if it happen to be the *shooting-season*, or he hath some bright-eyed *cousine* at home.

A fine time of it certainly, the man of pleasure has at the University; before his health is ruined, or his *reputation*, if indeed he has any care of that, be lost by being plucked, rusticated, or expelled; and, above all, before his credit, as his stay draws towards a close, is gone with the trades-people, and the daily, hourly, ever craving DUN stalks a grim sentinel before his door;—not but what this last " *atra cura*" is easily dismissed from the mind of the reckless boy, when removed from his sight or hearing.

Yet we have often suspected, that the idle jesting and ridicule on this point, of many of the youngsters is assumed to hide the conscious degradation of a proud spirit, writhing under petty persecution, and tormented by self-reproach. We hope that we are right.

Let us mention, and endeavour to account for,

before we conclude, a circumstance, which lately came to our knowledge. A gentleman, on whose veracity we rely, told us, that an eminent medical man had remarked to him, a short time ago, how many Oxford and Cambridge men* were tenants of *lunatic asylums ;* which he attributed to incessant cigar-smoking; so many Oxonians and Cantabs having a cigar or pipe between their lips all day and the greater part of the night. Although we are of opinion that smoking, like other things, may be abused until it becomes very pernicious, yet we attribute this sad circumstance to many other causes as well; for, alas! gambling, drinking, hunting, without funds to justify such an expense, billiards, rowing *to excess* on a river running through low and marshy grounds, and low debauchery of person and mind, excessive eating, blaspheming, and uttering with their lips that which pollutes them, are but too common amongst University men. And when we add to all this, frequent disappointments, heart-burnings, and irrecoverable ruin of fortune, and that their health is destroyed by another cause, too delicate for us to investigate, but which, in great measure, arises from part of

* Although, being acquainted personally with it, we have spoken of Oxford only, we doubt not but that almost all we have said applies to the Sister University.

the mistaken policy of the University, we cannot wonder at the remark above cited. We should, indeed, wonder if it were otherwise.

For our own part, we never see a fine young man, strong in health and full of integrity, ardour, life, and enthusiasm, going to reside at this place of abominations, without sighing; as we think of the probable alteration for the worse, that three or four years of college life will make in him.

And now, it is getting time for us to cease for a season our complaints, and lay aside our indignant pen.

We have, unflinchingly, exposed the truth; although we are aware of the storm, that is impending over our heads. " *Oui, la religion, les pré-* " *jugés, la violence, se réunissent constamment contre* " *celui qui ose penser et agir."*

O ye " Budge Doctors,"* *not* of the " Stoic fur," but who know so well how to combine the Cynic for others with the Epicurean for yourselves—Ye sacerdotal trainers of youth, ye *mysterious flamens* and *flaminal mysts,*† ye Masters of Arts but artless masters, and ye rubicund portly *recruiting sergeants* of the Church *Militant,*—spare us your just wrath and your holy indignation; since we have

---

* Milton.

† Myst, a word coined from μυστἠς: μυστήριον, a sacred thing.

thus dared to reveal the *arcana sacra* of your den of imposture, and, in removing the prophet-veil, have disclosed the grinning features of *Mokanna*. Spare us your hornet stings, although we have thus boldly attacked your nest. Alas! already we feel the scorpion-pointed arrows of your wrath.

Ἰώ μοί μοι, ἒ ἒ
Οἴστρου δ' ἄρδις χρίει μ' ἄπυρος
Κραδία δὲ φόβῳ φρένα λακτίζει. *

Spare us unfortunate, who would wage war, not with yourselves, but with your principles, your craft, your cunning, your intolerance, your hypocrisy, your fawning spirits, your injustice, and your heartlessness; and we promise, if we survive your indignation, in gratitude to omit the last of the thousand and one instances of your baseness, which we have in store.

* Æschylus, Prom. Vinct.

THE END.

EFFINGHAM WILSON, PRINTER, BISHOPSGATE-STREET WITHIN.

CPSIA information can be obtained
at www.ICGtesting.com
Printed in the USA
LVRC011836191218
601071LV00006B/30

Le Rossignol: Opera Comique En Un Acte

Gabriel Charles L'Attaignant

LE
ROSSIGNOL,

OPERA COMIQUE
EN UN ACTE,

DE MESSIEURS ******.

Repréſenté pour la premiere fois le 15 Septembre
1752, & jours ſuivans, juſqu'à la clôture du
Théâtre du Fauxbourg Saint Laurent ;

Et continué le 3 Février 1753, pour l'Ouverture
du Théâtre du Fauxbourg Saint Germain.

Le prix eſt de 24 ſols avec la Muſique.

A PARIS,

Chez DUCHESNE, Libraire, rue Saint Jacques,
au-deſſous de la Fontaine Saint-Benoît,
au Temple du Goût.

· M. DCC. LVI.
Avec Approbation & Privilége du Roi.

AVERTISSEMENT.

LE Roffignol eſt une de ces Piéces qui
plaiſent par le mérite de leur propre
fond : il n'y faut point chercher d'intri-
gue compoſée ; car ce n'eſt proprement
que le Conte original mis en action très-
ſimple , & aſſujetti aux bienſéances du
Théâtre ; auſſi les deux Auteurs de ce petit
Opera , loin d'être aſſez vains pour s'attri-
buer tout le ſuccès dont le Public l'a ho-
noré , reconnoiſſent de bonne foi n'y de-
voir prétendre d'autre part , que celle d'a-
voir aſſez bien rendu , au gré des connoiſ-
ſeurs , un ſujet agréable , & de s'y être atta-
chés , autant qu'il leur a été poſſible , à la
pureté du ſtile , & au choix des Airs.

A ij

ACTEURS.

LISETTE, *Amante de Colin*, Mlle ROSALINE.

COLIN, *Amant de Lisette*, M. DESCHAMPS,
& *ensuite* M. LA RUETTE.

LE PERE DE LISETTE,　　M. PARAN.

LA MERE DE LISETTE,　Mlle ROLAND.

MATHURINE, *Cousine de Lisette*,
Mlle DEVILLIERS.

THIBAUT, *Paysan*, M. L'ECLUSE,
& *ensuite* M. MARTIN.

La Scene est dans une Ferme attenant un bocage.

LE
ROSSIGNOL,
OPERA COMIQUE
EN UN ACTE.

SCENE PREMIERE.

Le Théâtre repréfente une Ferme attenant un bocage.

LISETTE, MATHURINE.

MATHURINE:

Air : *J'entends déja le bruit des armes.*

ON jour ma petite coufine ,
Je te trouve un air bien rêveur.

LISETTE.

Ah ! tu te trompes , Mathurine ,
Je fuis toûjours de même humeur.

A iij

MATHURINE.

Si c'eſt l'Amour qui te lutine ,
Quoi ! n'oſes-tu m'ouvrir ton cœur ?

LISETTE.

Air : 1. *Témoins de mon indifférence.*

Non , non, c'eſt à l'indifférence
Que je dois le bonheur & la paix de mes jours ;
N'exige point de moi de confidence ,
Je ne connois encor ni d'amans , ni d'amours.

MATHURINE.

Air : *Du haut en bas.*

A ta façon ,
Ma belle enfant , de te défendre ,
A ta façon ,
Tu redoublerois mon ſoupçon :
Tu dis cela d'un air ſi tendre
Que l'on ne pourroit ſe méprendre
A ta façon.

LISETTE.

Air : *Eſt-ç' que ça ſe demande ?*

Devine donc , ſi tu le veux ,
Ce que je n'oſe dire ....
Eh quoi ! Couſine , dans mes yeux
Ne ſçàurois-tu le lire ?

MATHURINE.

Qu'ils ſont fripons & pleins d'ardeur !

LISETTE.

Que ta malice eſt grande !

MATHURINE.

N'aurois-tu pas donné ton cœur ?

LISETTE.

Eſt-ç' que ça ſe demande ?

Air : *Gentille Pellerine.*

Suis-je donc si blâmable ?

MATHURINE.

Non, quand on est aimable,
L'amour est excusable,
Dans l'âge où te voilà.

LISETTE.

Comme souvent la vie
D'amertume est remplie,
Un Amant défennuye.

MATHURINE.

Oui dà, Lisette, oui dà,
Je crois ç'la
Propre au mal qui te tient là.

LISETTE.

Air : *Belle Iris, vous avez deux pommes.*
Maman me tient à la lisiere,
Je ne puis m'éloigner d'un pas :
Sitôt qu'elle ne me voit pas,
Elle crie, elle est en colere.
Du Rossignol j'aime la voix....
Je n'ose aller au bord du bois.

MATHURINE.

Air : *Bouchez, Nayades, vos fontaines.*
Ta mere a de l'expérience.

LISETTE.

D'où lui vient cette défiance ?

MATHURINE.

Que sçait-on ? Il peut arriver
Que tu t'égares de ta route :

A iv

Un loup venant à te trouver,
T'auroit bientôt croqué sans doute.
   Air : *Aie, aie, aie Jeannette.*
A quelques pas de chez-nous
Est une forêt touffue :
Moi qui ne crains point les loups,
Un jour j'en revins mordue,
    Aie, aie, aie.
     LISETTE.
Air : N°. 2. *Je ne vais point seulette au bois.*
Je ne vais point seulette aux bois,
Quand la nuit est obscure :
On y pourroit risquer, je crois,
Quelque triste aventure.
Colin m'escorte quelquefois.
    MATHURINE.
   Ce Berger te rassure.
    LISETTE.
   Air : *Mi mi fa re mi.*
Dans le bois tous deux ensemble
Qu'aurions-nous à redouter ?
    MATHURINE.
Quand l'Amour vous y rassemble
Est-ce bien pour écouter ?
   Mi mi fa re mi,
   Le chant si joli,
   Mi mi fa re sol,
   Du doux Rossignol.
    LISETTE.
Air : *A l'ombre de ce verd bocage.*
Que je me plais à son ramage !

MATHURINE.
Rien n'eſt ſi doux que ſes chanſons ;
On prétend que dans ſon langage
D'amour il dicte des leçons.

LISETTE.
Oui, je crois que ce Dieu l'inſpire,
Car auſſitôt qu'il forme un ſon,
Je ſoupire, Colin ſoupire,
Nous ſoupirons à l'Uniſſon.

MATHURINE.
Air : *Du haut en bas.*
A qui des deux
Donnerois-tu la préférence,
A qui des deux,
De ce Roſſignol amoureux,
Ou de Colin : en conſcience,
Dis ce que ton petit cœur penſe,
A qui des deux ?

LISETTE.
Air : *Ah ! que ma voix me devient chere !*
Le Roſſignol chante à merveille,
Mais le chant de Colin me ſemble plus flateur.

MATHURINE.
Le chant du Roſſignol eſt ſi plein de douceur !

LISETTE.
Ses ſons me ſéduiſent l'oreille,
Mais ceux de Colin vont au cœur.

MATHURINE.
Air : *Rions, chantons, amuſons-nous.*
Je vois le Berger qui t'engage,
Vous allez chanter un duo :

Adieu , Coufine ; le trio
A Cythere n'eſt pas d'uſage :
Riez , chantez , amuſez-vous ,
Il n'eſt point de plaiſir plus doux.   ] *bis.*

SCENE II.

LISETTE *feule , apercevant Colin de loin.*

Air : *Quand on a prononcé.*

COLIN ne me voit pas , écoutons-le en ca-
            chette ,
Il va s'entretenir de ſa flâme ſecrette :
Ah ! qu'il me ſera doux d'entendre que ſon cœur
Brûle toûjours pour moi d'une ſincere ardeur !

SCENE III.

COLIN *feul , & Liſette à ſon tour dans
l'éloignement.*

Air : *Quand vous entendrez le doux* Zéphir.

QUE pour mon cœur ces lieux ont d'attraits ;
    Lorſque j'y vois celle que j'adore !
Le Dieu d'Amour qui la ſuit de près
        Les embellit encore :
        Ces fleurs , ces eaux ,
        Le chant des oiſeaux ,

Le souffle volage
Du tendre Zéphir,
Ce verd feuillage,
Ce doux ombrage,
Tout peint le plaisir :
Dès qu'elle part, la fleur se flétrit,
Le Rossignol cesse son ramage :
La seule Tourterelle gémit
Dans ce triste bocage.

Appercevant Lisette qui s'avance vers lui.

Air : *La mort de mon cher pere.*
Ah ! c'est toi, ma Lisette !

LISETTE.
Ah ! Colin, c'est donc vous !
Que je suis satisfaite !

COLIN.
Que mon destin est doux !
Quand je tiens ma Bergere
Seulette en ce séjour,
Je me crois à Cythere
Dans les bras de l'Amour.

LISETTE.
Air : *Ah ! que la paresseuse Automne !*
Ce n'est pas sans soins & sans peine
Que j'échappe aux yeux surveillans :
Quand près de toi l'Amour m'amene,
Je fais accroire à mes parens
Que je ne viens dans ce bocage,
Que pour entendre les accens
Du Rossignol, dont le ramage
Fait tous mes plaisirs innocens.

Air : *Nous fommes précepteurs d'amour.*

Ils penfent que ce feul defir
Chaque jour m'engage à m'y rendre :
Mais j'ai cent fois plus de plaifir
De t'y trouver que de l'entendre.

COLIN.

Air : *L'autre jour étant affis.*
Qu'un aveu fi plein d'appas
Répand de feux dans mon ame !
Et comment mon cœur, hélas !
Suffit-il à tant de flâme.

LISETTE.

Que le mien eft content !
Mais feras-tu fidele ?

COLIN.

Pour faire un inconftant
Ma Lifette eft trop belle.

Air : *Babet, que t'es gentille !*
Je n'eus jamais deffein,
Lifon, de te féduire :
Tout ce que dit Colin,
C'eft l'Amour qui l'infpire.
Oui, fi j'étois Roi,
J'en jure ma foi,
Mon fceptre & ma couronne
Dès cet inftant feroient ton bien :
Mon tréfor deviendroit le tien :
Mais hélas ! à moi je n'ai rien
Qu'un cœur, je te le donne.   *bis.*

LISETTE.
Même Air.

Quoi ! peut-on être épris
D'une vaine richeffe !
Je connois tout le prix ,
Berger , de ta tendreffe.
    N'es-tu pas mon Roi ?
    Cher Colin , en toi
Ce n'eft que toi que j'aime,
Non , les grandeurs n'ajoûtent rien
A l'amant , quand on aime bien :
Prends mon cœur , donne-moi le tien :
    Voilà le bien fuprême.
        Ici le Roffignol chante.

Air : *Vous qui donnez de l'amour.*

Ah ! Colin , en ce moment
Le Roffignol chante ;
Que fa voix m'enchante !
Ah ! Colin , en ce moment
Le Roffignol chante ;
Quel raviffement !

    COLIN.

Tu voudrois bien le tenir ?

    LISETTE.

Hélas ! c'eft tout mon defir.

    Air : *Voici les Dragons.*

Mais de loin je vois ma mere ,
    Vîte cache-toi :
Va , je ne tarderai guere ,
Cher Colin , à m'en défaire ,
    Laiffe-moi.

SCENE IV.

LISETTE *seule.*

Air : N°. 7. *Avec l'aimable Dorine.*

DEs sons de sa voix légere,
Ce Rossignol plein d'amour
Fait retentir nuit & jour
Cet asyle solitaire ;
Qu'il y goûte de plaisirs !
Hélas ! il n'a point de mere,
Qui condamne ses soupirs
Et s'oppose à ses desirs.

SCENE V.

LE PERE , LA MERE , LISETTE.

LA MERE.

Air : *Des Trembleurs.*

EST-CE ainsi qu'on me balotte ?
Comment donc , petite sotte ,
Il faut qu'après vous je trotte ,
Et vous cherche à tous instans ?
M'obéit-on de la sorte ?
J'ai beau défendre qu'on sorte ,

A peine on ouvre la porte,
Vous prenez la clef des champs.

LISETTE.

Air : *On n'aime point dans nos Forêts.*
Pardon, Maman, je ne vois pas
Quel est le sujet qui vous fâche ;
Seule je ne puis faire un pas,
Je suis comme un chien à l'attache....
J'avois besoin de prendre l'air.

LA MERE.

Dans ce besoin je vois trop clair.
Air : *Ah ! mon mal ne vient que d'aimer.*
Vraiment, vraiment, nous y voilà....
Je connois tous ces besoins-là ;
Une fille toûjours en a :
Ma petite mignonne,
Pour donner dans ce paneau-là,
Je ne suis pas si bonne.

LE PERE.

Air : *Il faut que je file.*
Je vous trouve trop sévere,
S'il faut parler sans détour.

LISETTE.

Ai-je si grand tort, ma mere,
Quand il arrive un beau jour,
D'aller faire, faire, faire,
D'aller faire un petit tour ?

LE PERE.

Air : *Si tu veux être affable.*
Elle a raison, soit dit sans vous déplaire,
On peut gronder, c'est le droit d'une mere,

Mais
L'exercice eſt néceſſaire,
Vous la tenez de trop près.

LA MERE.

Air : *Robin, turelure.*

De grace, mon cher époux,
Taiſez-vous, je vous conjure :
Je connois bien mieux que vous.

LE PERE.

Turelure.

LA MERE.

Les beſoins de la nature.

LE PERE.

Robin, turelure lure.

LA MERE.

Air : *Du Prevôt des Marchands.*

'où veniez-vous hier au ſoir ?
nme en un four il faiſoit noir ;
z, petite impertinente.

LISETTE.

nois du petit bois,
harmant Roſſignol chante ;
rien tant que ſa voix.

MERE.

got *ſur la brune.*
ntaiſie !
-e manie !
aiſie !
n chaud ;
-e,
?

Pauvre

Pauvre pecore ,
Pour un oifeau ,
Rifquer un rhume de cerveau !
LISETTE.
Air : *Ah ! le bel oifeau !*
Ah ! le bel oifeau , Maman !
Qu'il eft d'un joli plumage !
Ah ! le bel oifeau , Maman !
Et qu'il chante joliment !
C'eft tout mon amufement
Que d'entendre fon ramage :
Que ne puis-je , oifeau charmant ,
Te prendre & te mettre en cage ?
Ab ! le bel oifeau , Maman !
Qu'il eft d'un joli plumage ,
Ah le bel oifeau , Maman ,
Et qu'il chante joliment !
LE PERE.
Air : *N'y a pas d' mal à ça.*
Pourquoi lui défendre
Ce paffe-tems-là ?
Elle peut l'entendre
Tant qu'elle voudra ,
N'y a pas d' mal à ça.   *bis.*
LISETTE.
Air : *Les Triolets.*
J'avois prefque la main deffus ,
Un jour que j'étois au bocage ,
Quand deux manans font accourus ,
J'avois prefque la main deffus ;
Au bruit qu'ont fait ces malotrus ,
B

Il s'eft envolé , quel dommage !
J'avois prefque la main deffus.

LE PERE.

Tu l'aurois attrapé , je gage.

LISETTE.

Air : *Nannette , dormez-vous ?*
Je croyois le tenir ,   *bis.*
Quand je le vis partir ,
Jugez quel déplaifir !
On enrage beaucoup
Quand on manque fon coup,

LA MERE.

Air : *Contre mon gré je chéris l'eau.*
Finiffons tous ces propos là.

LE PERE.

Mon Dieu, ma femme, laiffez-la...
Va , ma chere enfant, va l'entendre ,
Ton plaifir eft bien naturel ;
Et mets-lui , fi tu veux le prendre ,
Deffus la queuë un grain de fel.

Air : *Je fuis la fleur.*
Je veux qu'aux bois Mathurine te fuive ,
Pour t'aider à le dénicher.

LISETTE.

Y fongez-vous ? Ma Coufine eft trop vive ,
Elle pourroit l'effaroucher.

LA MERE.

Air : *Quel homme êtes-vous.*
Toujours indulgent ,
Vraiment voilà comme
On gâte un enfant :

Votre bonté m'assomme.
Ah ! mon pauvre époux ,
Quel homme , quel homme ,
Ah ! mon pauvre époux ,
Quel homme êtes-vous ?

Le Pere & la Mere s'en vont.

SCENE VI.

LISETTE *seule.*

Air : *Dam' me voilà.*

ME voici libre de tout soin ,
Et de fâcheux témoin
    Loin :
Profitons de ce doux moment ,
Rapellons vîte mon Amant :
Colin , Colin , que n'es-tu là ?

SCENE VII.

LISETTE , COLIN *arrive en courant , & acheve l'air.*

COLIN.

DAm' me voilà , me voilà là.
B ij

Air : *Nous nous marierons Dimanche.*
Derriere un buiſſon
J'attendois Liſon ,
Que mon bonheur eſt extrême !
ENSEMBLE.
Toujours t'aimer ,
Et t'enflamer
De même.
LISETTE.
C'eſt mon deſir.
COLIN.
C'eſt mon plaiſir
Suprême.
ENSEMBLE.
Uniſſons nos voix ,
Répétons cent fois :
Qu'on eſt heureux , quand on aime !
COLIN.

Air : N°. 8. *Muſette d'Ajax.*
Toi , dont le ramage tendre
Fait le charme de ces bois ,
Roſſignol fais-nous entendre
Les doux accens de ta voix ;
De l'Amour chante les flâmes ,
Et juſqu'au fond de nos ames
Porte le feu de tes ſoupirs ,
Puiſſions-nous dans ce bocage
Si propice à nos deſirs ,
Comme toi , ſous cet ombrage ,
Bientôt chanter nos plaiſirs !

LISETTE.

Air : 4. *Maman , qu'eſt-ce donc qu'ils faiſoient ?*

Ah ! que ne puis-je à la maiſon
Tenir ce Roſſignol aimable ?
De ſon goſier le joli ſon
Me rendroit la vie agréable :

COLIN.

Il chanteroit ,
S'animeroit
D'une façon ſi tendre ,
Que ton plus doux plaiſir ſeroit
De le voir & l'entendre.

LISETTE.

Air : *Ah ! qu'il eſt beau l'oiſeau !*
Mais en cage quand il ſera ,   *bis.*
Crois-tu que ce bel oiſeau-là
Que j'aime , que j'aime ,
Cher Colin , chantera
Toujours de même ?

COLIN.

Air : 5. *Je n'entends plus deſſous l'ormeau.*

Oui , ma Bergere , il chérira
Toujours ſon eſclavage ,
Jamais le tems n'affoiblira
Son feu ni ſon ramage :
Et ce Roſſignol chantant ſi bien ,
Te prouvera dans ſon langage ,
Qu'à notre âge
L'amour eſt le vrai bien.

B iij

COLIN & LISETTE.

Air : *Dès aujourd'hui , si tu me crois.*
Dès aujourd'hui , si tu me crois
Il faut tâcher de le surprendre :
Bon *, voilà qu'il se fait entendre
Au fond du bois.

COLIN.

Air : *Maman me dit que je suis ignorante.*
Belle Lison, sans tarder davantage ,
Dans les taillis , je cours te le chercher ;
Fût-il couvert du plus épais feuillage ,
Bientôt Colin sçaura le dénicher.

LISETTE.

Air : *Les Dieux comptent nos jours.*
Sans moi tu veux aller : cher Colin , il me semble
Que je te dois aider , dans un projet si beau.
Attens-moi donc ,   *bis.*
Pour ne pas manquer notre oiseau ,
Il faut partir ensemble.

Ils s'en vont d'un côté , & on voit arriver de l'autre les
Acteurs de la Scene suivante.

* Ici le Rossignol chante dans l'éloignement.

═══════════════════════════════

SCENE VIII.
LE PERE , LA MERE , MATHURINE ,
THIBAUT.
MATHURINE.
Air : *Mariez , mariez moi.*
MA tante , permettez-vous
Que je parle avec franchise ?
Lison. . . . .

LA MERE.

Hé bien ?

MATHURINE.

Entre-nous ,

De Colin , me semble éprise ,

Mariez , mariez , mariez la ,

De peur de quelque surprise ,

Mariez , mariez , mariez la .

Car elle vous préviendra.

THIBAUT.

Air : *Adieu paniers.*

Je la trouvai dans ces retraites

L'autre jour seule avec Colin ,

MATHURINE.

Elle est rusée , il est malin.

THIBAUT.

Et l'air du bois est fatal aux fillettes.

MATHURINE.

Air : *De tous les Capucins du monde.*

Oh ! franchement de sa poupée ,

Elle n'est plus guere occupée.

THIBAUT.

Je la vis portant des gluaux ,

Et légerement équipée ;

Sans doute c'étoient des oiseaux

Qu'elle alloit prendre à la pipée.

Air : *Un Abbé dans un coin.*

De l'œil je la suivis ,

Et je vis

Qu'à terre elle avoit mis ,

Au bord d'une tranchée

B iv.

Quelques petits filets,
Et qu'elle étoit cachée
Comme un chat aux aguets.
　　　Air : *Jardinier ne vois-tu pas ?*
Elle n'agiffoit non plus
Qu'un idole de marbre,
Et dans l'inftant j'apperçus
Que Colin étoit deffus
　　　Un arbre.
　　　　　Même Air.
Là, fans doute, il n'étoit pas
Pour enfiler des perles ;
Car il y tendoit des lacs,
Et je vis tomber en bas
　　Des Merles.
　　MATHURINE.
Air : *Sçavez-vous bien, Beauté cruelle ?*
Je les vois s'amufer enfemble
Tous les jours à de petits jeux :
Mais ces jeux-là, que vous en femble ?
Ne font-ils pas quelquefois dangereux ?
Colin, au jeu, m'a tout l'air d'être heureux.
　　　LA MERE.
Il n'eft que trop vrai, Dieux ! je tremble.
　　　LE PERE.
Air : *Nous vivons dans l'innocence.*
Honni foit, qui mal y penfe,
Ah ! quelle malignité !
Ce font plaifirs de l'enfance
Et pleins de fimplicité,
Qui prouvent leur innocence
Et leur ingénuité.

THIBAUT.

Air: N°. 6. *Point de bruit.*

Point de bruit, bouche clofe,
Je vois,
Je crois,
Quelque chofe,
Point de bruit, bouche clofe,
Les voici
Tout près d'ici :
C'eft Colin
Et Lifette,
Le badin !
La folette !
Comme ils s'amufent entr'eux !
Les voyez-vous bien tous deux ?

MATHURINE.

Air : *Ne v'la-t-il pas que j'aime ?*

Que tête à tête on eft heureux
Avec l'objet qu'on aime !

THIBAUT.

Lorfque l'on croît n'être que deux,
L'Amour fait le troifiéme.

LE PERE *après avoir regardé au travers du feuillage.*

Air : *Ah ! j'ai tout vû.*

Ah ! qu'ai-je vû ?
L'ai-je bien apperçu ?
C'eft Lifon, qui l'eût cru ?
Ah ! qu'ai-je vû ?
Son cœur eft prévenu.
Hélas ! tout eft perdu :
Ma femme, qu'en dis-tu ?

LA MERE.

J'avois prévu
Qu'en souffrant que Lisette,
Au bois fût seulette,
Elle en abuseroit,
Et nous attraperoit :

ENSEMBLE.

Ah ! qu'ai-je vû ?
Son cœur est prévenu.
Hélas ! tout est perdu :
Ma femme, ⎤
Mon mari, ⎦ qu'en dis-tu ?

LA MERE.

Air : *Est-il de plus douces odeurs ?*

Prenons notre parti soudain,
Puisque la faute est faite :
Lisette est faite pour Colin,
Et Colin pour Lisette.

LE PERE.

Nous les surprenons en ces lieux :
Qu'un doux nœud les assemble.
Que pouvons-nous faire de mieux ?
Marions-les ensemble.

SCENE IX. & derniere.

LISETTE *fortant du bois avec* COLIN, *les Acteurs de la Scene précédente.*

LISETTE *tenant un Roffignol dans une cage.*

Air : *Allez-vous-en, gens de la nôce.*

JE tiens cet oifeau qui m'enchante ,
Enfin le Roffignol eft pris :
Que ma mere fera contente !
Je ne bougerai du logis ,
Et n'irai plus fous le taillis ;
Je tiens cet oifeau qui m'enchante ,
Enfin le Roffignol eft pris.

LE PERE & LA MERE , *à Lifette & à Colin.*
Air : *Dans ce féjour.*

Tendres amans ,
Soyez contens :
Hymen , Amour ,
Pour vous en ce jour,
Joignent leurs feux
Et leurs nœuds.

LISETTE & COLIN.
Dieux !

LISETTE *feule.*

Ah , mon pere ! ah , maman !
Quel bonheur , quel plaifir , quel moment !
Cher Colin ,
Puis-je enfin

Te nommer librement
Mon Amant ?
LE PERE & LA MERE.
De ces oifeaux ,
Dont vous trouviez les chants fi beaux ,
Imitez les jeux ,
Soyez encor plus heureux
Qu'eux.

COLIN *à Lifette.*
Air : *Printems dans nos bocages.*
Ma mie ,
Ah ! que j'envie
Le fort de ton oifeau !
Sans ceffe ,
Quelque careffe :
Que fon deftin eft beau !
Qu'il doit être heureux ,
S'il fent le prix de ta tendreffe ,
Qu'il doit être heureux !
C'eft où je borne tous mes vœux :
Ma mie ,
Ah ! que j'envie
Le fort de ton oifeau !
Sans ceffe ,
Quelque careffe :
Que fon deftin eft beau !
Air : *La Bourgogne , Fanfare.*
La plus aimable Bergere
Vient de recevoir ma foi :
Ah ! qu'il eft doux de lui plaire ,
Et de vivre fous fa loi !

COLIN & LISETTE *ensemble.*
A la chaîne qui nous lie ,
Je me livre sans retour ,
Et perdrai plutôt la vie ,
Que de perdre mon amour.
Second Couplet.
LISETTE.
Que de tendres chansonnettes
Annoncent notre bonheur :
COLIN.
Que le son de nos musettes
Soit d'accord avec le cœur :
ENSEMBLE.
Chantons l'Amour & ses flâmes :
Le chanter est un plaisir ,
Qui doit préparer nos ames
A celui de le servir.
LE PERE.
Air : *Ça n'dur'ra pas toujours.*
Que la nôce commence ,
C'est le tems des amours :
Il est juste qu'on danse
Au plus beau de ses jours ;
Car on n'dans' pas toujours ;
Car , &c.

COUPLET

Inferé dans le DIVERTISSEMENT.

COLIN.

Air : *Dans ce féjour la paix & l'innocence.*

CHarmans oifeaux de ce riant bocage,
Chantez, chantez, redoublez vos concèrts ;
Par vos accens, rendez un jufte hommage
A la Beauté dont je porte les fers :
Le Dieu des ris & des tendres alarmes,
Entr'elle & moi partage fa faveur ;
A ma Bergere il donne tous fes charmes,
Et réunit tous fes traits dans mon cœur.

Air : Noté N°. 9.

Fiers Roffignols, l'ornement de nos bois,
    Ne vantés plus votre ramage :   ] *bis.*
Non, non, ne vantés plus votre langage :
Nous imitons la douceur de votre voix,
    Et furpaffons votre ramage :
Nous imitons la douceur de votre voix,
Et furpaffons votre ramage.
Fiers Roffignols, &c.

VAUDEVILLE.

LI- fon, quel plaifir de te voir, Et d'enten-

dre ton doux ra-ma- ge! Que Colin eft heu-

reux d'a-voir Un pa-reil Roffignol en ca- ge!

2.

Vous connoiffez ce Financier,
Qui fait un fi grand étalage ;
Dès demain quelque créancier
Mettra ce Roffignol en cage.

3.

On dit qu'on foupe après le jeu,
Chez Cloris, dans le voifinage :
Son fouper lui coûte bien peu,
Elle a des Roffignols en cage.

4.

D'une Chanteufe d'Opera,
Lubin entretient le ménage ;
Ne peut-on pas dire qu'il a
Un joli Roffignol en cage.

5.

Orgon ce vieux mari jaloux,
Qui connoît le fexe volage,
Met fa femme fous les verroux,
Et tient le Roffignol en cage.

6.

Meffieurs, l'Auteur met fon efpoir
Dans l'honneur de votre fuffrage ;
S'il l'obtient, venez tous revoir
Souvent le Roffignol en cage.

F I N.

APPROBATION.

J'AI lû par ordre de Monfeigneur le Chancelier, *Le R*
fignol, *Opera-Comique*, & je crois que l'on peut en p
mettre la reprefentation & l'impreffion. A Paris, cc
Septembre 1752.   CREBILLON.

Le Privilège & l'enregiftrement fe trouvent à la fin
tome 3e. du Nouveau Recueil des Piéces reprefentées fur
Théâtre de l'Opéra-Comique depuis fon rétabliffement, &
AIRS CHOIS.

CPSIA information can be obtained
at www.ICGtesting.com
Printed in the USA
LVIC06n0216250717
542534LV00007B/69